dedication

I would like to dedicate the photography in this book to those who encouraged me to pursue this field — my sister Lois Arthurs and her husband, Mario Cappelli; my dear son, John, who loves books and Mom's photos; and most of all, Chet, my husband of 48 years, without whose support I would never have sold my first picture. To my friends Patty Anderson and Hui Zhang I extend my heartfelt thanks for their assistance in preparing for my art shows.

A special memorial dedication is for my sweet daughter, Beth Ann, who died of leukemia at the age of eleven. How blessed I am to have captured much of her life on film! — *Agnes L. Barnes, Photographer*

S cott would like to dedicate this book to his wife Marilyn, his daughters Amelia and Sara, and Marilyn's daughters Allyson and Gayle. They are an ongoing source of inspiration and blessings.

introduction

The idea for "Choosing the Gift" came out of Scott's work with people who had lost loved ones. He noticed that the ones who did not cope very well with the loss of a loved one were the ones who could not get past focusing on the loss itself. On the other hand, those who did move through their grief were the ones who focused on the emotional and spiritual gifts their loved one gave to them and in many ways were still giving to them.

After writing the words for the book approximately ten years before the actual publication, Scott began looking for an artist or photographer to make the words come alive. After a few false starts with various artists, the book was put on hold for about ten years, though it was never far from Scott's mind.

Enter Agnes and Chet Barnes.

Actually, Scott had met Chet years earlier while doing some substance abuse training for high school counselors. When Chet became aware that Scott had also done bereavement work, he spoke to him about the loss of his and Agnes' daughter, Beth Ann, to leukemia. They helped start a support group for parents who had lost children and asked if Scott would speak to them. The courage and hope and leadership of Chet and Agnes were actually part of the inspiration for the book.

During the following years Agnes became an incredible award winning photographer. Scott would run into her and Chet at various artists' exhibitions, but it wasn't until Chet and Agnes came to a book signing for another of Scott's books did it dawn on him to mention "Choosing the Gift" as a possible collaboration between Agnes and him. Not only did it have possibilities artistically, but considering the combination of their experiences with loss it seemed like a perfect match. This book shows the wisdom of that choice. It was a labor of love and reflects the deep belief of both Agnes and Scott that people can move past their grief and not only celebrate the lives of those who have gone before, but take their gifts and touch countless others as they move through life.

choosing the gift

hen someone you love dies
the path of your life
s forever changed

that path —

which so recently was filled

with the warmth and vitality

of your loved one

now seems strange
and frightening

a hole exists

where there once was
life

choosing the gift

the emptiness
seems without bottom

pain, anger, fear, confusion
crowd in and slowly begin
to overwhelm your senses

isolation and loneliness
surround you

choosing the gift

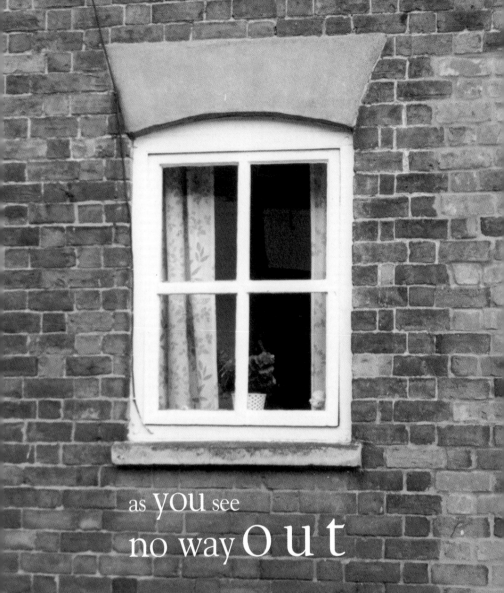

as you see
no way o u t

perhaps you hear the voices of friends

calling you on the wind

perhaps you see them

beckoning to you,

but your way is blocked

Storms pound the path

and your heart

perhaps you run wildly

through this
strange land

choosing the gift

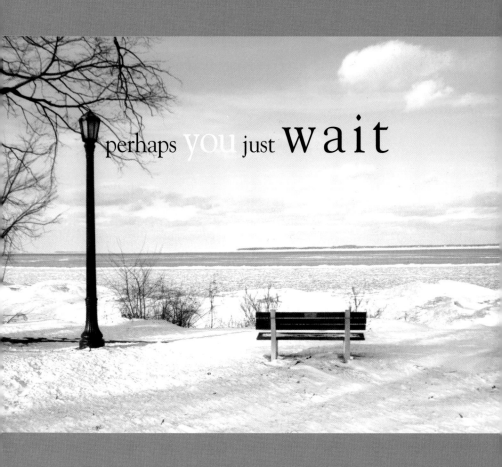

perhaps you just wait

any moment you know
you will be

devoured

choosing the gift

by this n i g h t m a r e

but

you aren't

and then... something begins to stir in you

it is what you call it ...

god... life... love... strength

choosing the gift

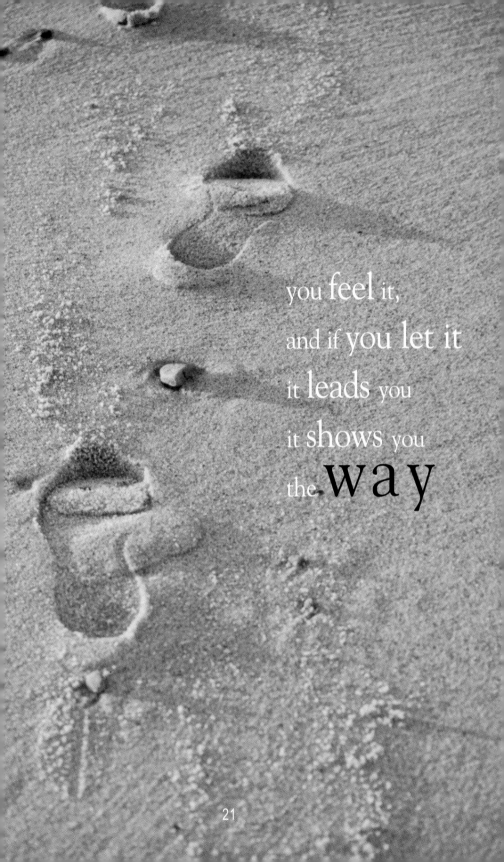

you feel it,
and if you let it
it leads you
it shows you
the way

slowly,
almost imperceptibly,

you begin to see the path again

choosing the gift

and though it still hurts,

you begin to realize

that the path itself is a gift

and that your loved one was

and continues to be

an ongoing gift

little by little

the path begins

to shine again

the chasm is still there —

the chasm will always be there

but now you know at your deepest level

you are faced with a choice

you can focus on the chasm...

or

you can focus on the gifts
your loved one brought —
and in fact still brings

to the path

choosing the gift

choosing the gift

if you focus on the chasm,

the path and your loved one's

gifts will disappear

and the bottomless hole

will dominate your life

if you focus on the gifts

of your loved one

(though tears will be shed from time to time)

the joy of these gifts

will fill your life

and you will share these gifts

with others on their paths

choosing the gift

and the beauty of your loved one's life and spirit

choosing the gift

will travel endless paths

and touch countless hearts

choosing the gift

as long as time exists

Agnes' interest in photography began with the gift of a camera when she was in high school and continued through her years of marriage and child rearing. After the death of her daughter in 1980, she used the medium of photo slides of Beth Ann's life in conducting seminars and presentations for church, educational and medical groups to portray ways to assist families with chronically or terminally ill children. She and her husband, Chet, were involved in starting a support group for bereaved parents shortly after Beth Ann's death, and they facilitated the group for ten years.

The photographs of Agnes L. Barnes speak to the heart and come in a wide variety of subjects which appeal to a diverse audience. She and Chet have traveled extensively in the United States, as well as to many countries, including England, Europe, South Africa, and Pohnpei and other islands in the Pacific Ocean.

Agnes has been selling at outdoor art shows since 1995. Whether you want a beautiful scenic picture for your living room, a nostalgic image to remind you of the past, or a college photograph for a recent graduate, Agnes has a fine selection of eye-catching photos from which to choose.

Dr. Sheperd has a B.A. in Music, a Master's Degree in Mass Communication, and a Ph.D. in Counseling. In addition to conducting very well received workshops and seminars for professionals in the fields of business, health care and education, Dr. Sheperd has produced a variety of hands-on material. He is co-author of "Cancer and Hope, (now titled The Healing Journey)," and "I Will Live Today," books for the seriously ill.

He has recently completed a book called "Who's In Charge?" — Attacking the Stress Myth. His book "What Do You Think Of You?," is on self-esteem for young people and their parents. His "The Survival Handbook for the Newly Recovering," focuses on substance abuse. He also has had produced on stage a musical play called "The Journey" that focuses on the power of the human spirit.

Additional books can be purchased at Dr. Sheperd's web site — www.mystressdr.com

choosing the gift